Easy Crafts in **5** Steps

Easy Clay Crafts
in 5 Steps

Enslow Elementary
an imprint of
Enslow Publishers, Inc.

40 Industrial Road
Box 398
Berkeley Heights, NJ 07922
USA
http://www.enslow.com

T0002184

Note to Teachers and Parents: Crafts are prepared using air-drying clay. Please follow package directions. Children may use color clay or they may paint using poster paint once clay is completely dry. The colors used in this book are suggestions. Children may use any color clay, cardboard, pencils, or paint they wish. Let them use their imaginations!

Enslow Elementary, an imprint of Enslow Publishers, Inc.
Enslow Elementary ® is a registered trademark of Enslow Publishers, Inc.

Translated from the Spanish edition by Ian Grenzeback, edited by Jaime Ramirez-Castilla, of Strictly Spanish, LLC. Edited and produced by Enslow Publishers, Inc.

Library of Congress Cataloging-in-Publication Data

Llimós Plomer, Anna.
    [Barro. English]
    Easy clay crafts in 5 steps / Anna Llimós.
        p. cm. — (Easy crafts in 5 steps)
    Summary: "Presents clay art projects that can be made in 5 steps"—Provided by publisher.
    Includes bibliographical references and index.
    ISBN-13: 978-0-7660-3085-5
    ISBN-10: 0-7660-3085-7
    1. Pottery craft —Juvenile literature. I. Title. II. Title: Easy clay crafts in five steps.
    TT920.L56 2007
    738.1'42—dc22
                            2007000750

Originally published in Spanish under the title *Barro*.
Copyright © 2005 PARRAMÓN EDICIONES, S.A., - World Rights.
Published by Parramón Ediciones, S.A., Barcelona, Spain.
Text and development of the exercises: Anna Llimós
Photographs: Nos & Soto

Printed in Spain

10 9 8 7 6 5 4 3 2 1

Contents

Crafty Crab

MATERIALS

Tan, white, and black clay
Roller
Plastic Knife

1 With the roller or your hands, flatten the tan clay like a pancake.

2 Draw and cut a triangle out of the flat piece of clay.

3 Beginning with the base, roll the triangle to get the shape shown in the picture. Turn over the ends a little bit.

4 Place the piece as shown in the picture and draw a mouth with the tip of the plastic knife.

5 For the eyes, make two balls of white clay. Place black clay on them for pupils. Place them above the mouth and let them dry.

Space Creature

MATERIALS

Clay
Plastic Knife
Different colors of paint
Paintbrush

1 Mold a piece of clay into the shape of a head and body. Separate the legs by cutting them apart, and form the feet.

2 Add clay to make the belly, and mark the belly button with a plastic knife. Use the plastic knife to make the toes.

3 To make the arms, mold two rolls of clay, flatten them, and make the fingers. Attach them to the body.

4 Make two antennas and a trumpet nose out of clay. Attach them to the head.

5 Once the space creature is dry, paint the hands, feet, mouth, belly button, trumpet nose, antennas, and eyes.

Cat

MATERIALS

Clay
Roller
Plastic Knife
Different colors of paint
Paintbrush

1 Make a flat piece of clay and cut out a long rectangle.

2 Bend the rectangle into the shape of an upside down "U" (the cat's body). Smooth it together, leaving some for the feet. Mark the toes and the lines on the body with the plastic knife.

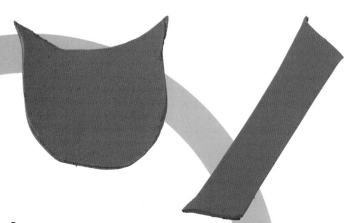

3 Make a thin flat piece of clay. Draw and cut out the cat's face and tail.

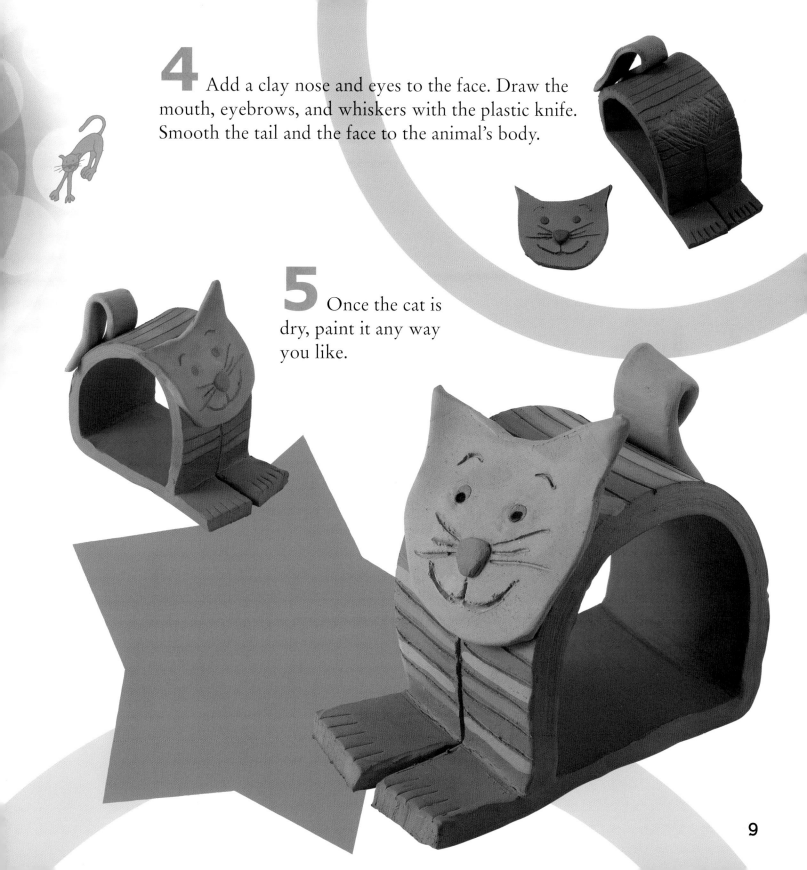

4 Add a clay nose and eyes to the face. Draw the mouth, eyebrows, and whiskers with the plastic knife. Smooth the tail and the face to the animal's body.

5 Once the cat is dry, paint it any way you like.

Pear-Shaped Box

MATERIALS

Clay
Plastic knife
Plastic spoon
Toothpick
Different colors of paint
Paintbrush

1 Mold a piece of clay into the shape of a pear.

2 Cut the top part off with the plastic knife.

3 Use a plastic spoon to take the clay out from the inside of the pear. Leave it empty.

4 Place a small roll of clay (the stem) on the top. Make a leaf out of clay and attach it to the stem with half a toothpick.

5 Once both parts are dry, paint the pear any way you like.

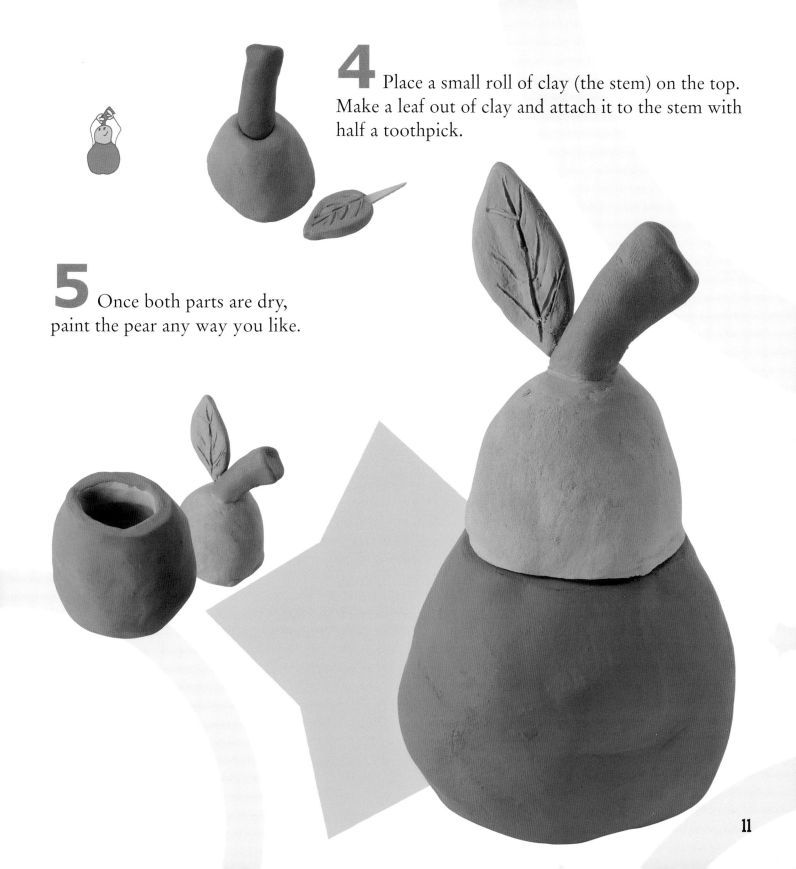

Letter Holder

1 Make one big square and two small rectangles out of a flattened piece of clay.

2 Draw the outline of five pencils on the square. Cut out around the pencils.

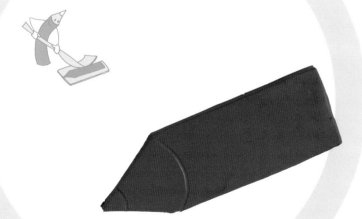

3 Draw an outline of a pencil on a rectangle and cut it out.

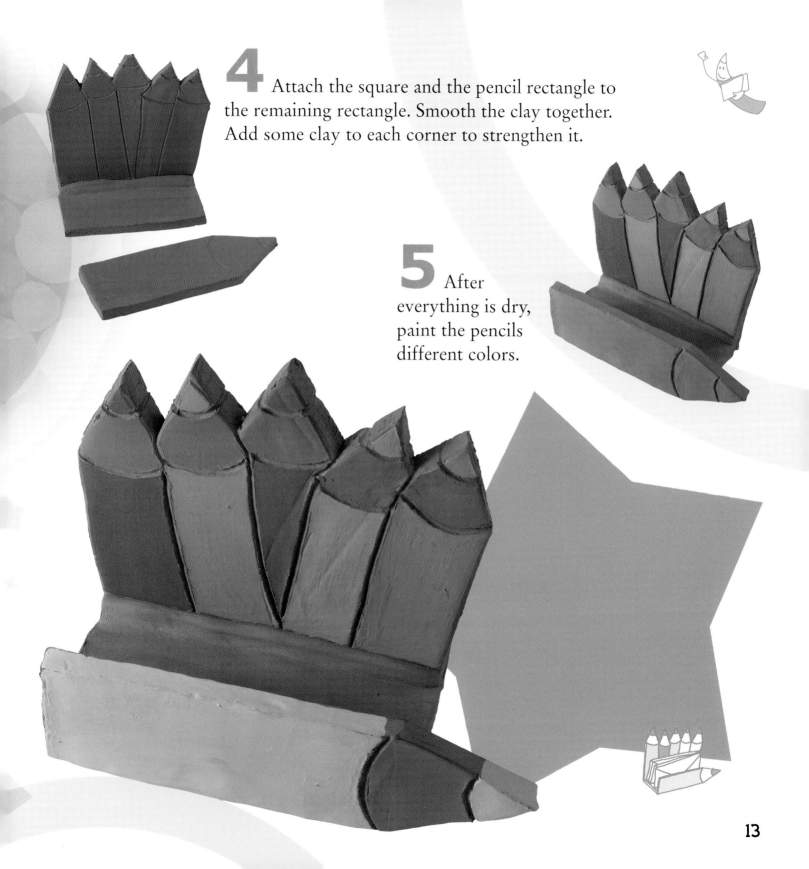

4 Attach the square and the pencil rectangle to the remaining rectangle. Smooth the clay together. Add some clay to each corner to strengthen it.

5 After everything is dry, paint the pencils different colors.

13

Inuit Igloo

MATERIALS

Clay
Plastic Knife
Different colors of paint
Paintbrush

1 For the igloo, make a half-sphere of clay. Make a small arch out of flattened clay. Attach the arch to the half-sphere.

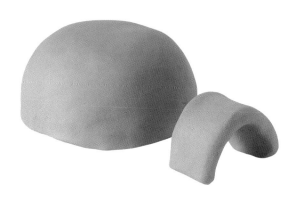

2 Draw the shape of ice blocks around the igloo with a plastic knife, and let it dry.

3 For the figure, make the body, feet, and head out of clay.

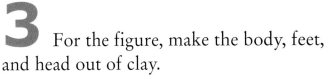

4 Use a plastic knife to make the eyes, nose, and mouth, and to draw marks for the fur.

5 Let the figure dry. Paint it as you like.

15

Snake

1 Make a long roll out of clay with one end wider than the other.

2 Give it the twisting shape of a snake with its head up. Open the mouth with the plastic knife.

3 For the eyes, make two balls of clay. Place pupils of clay on them. Place them on the head. Paint the pupils any color you wish.

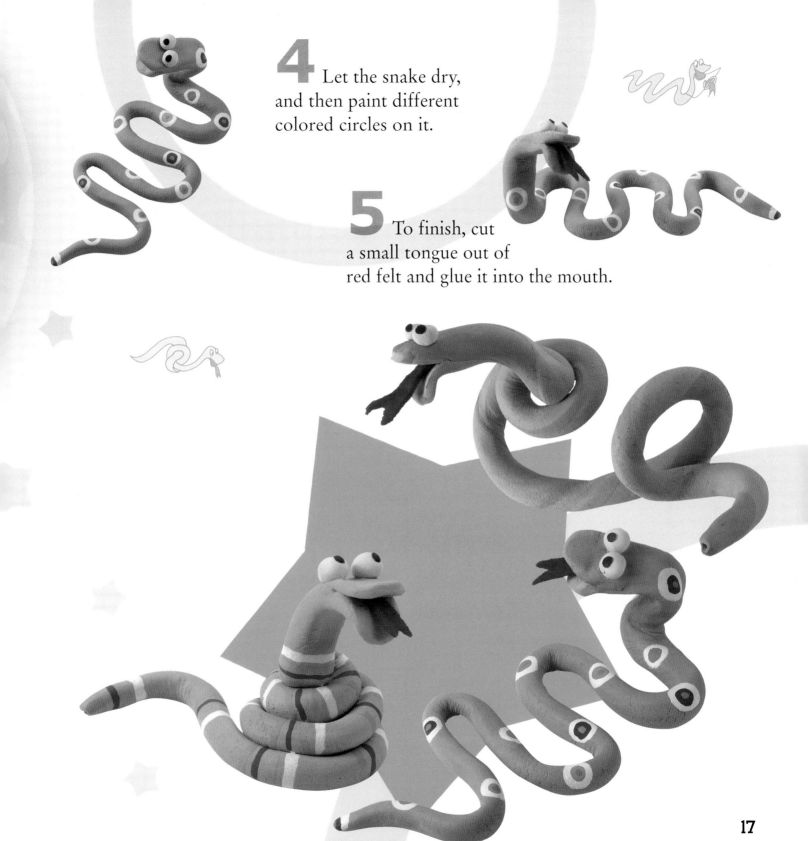

4 Let the snake dry, and then paint different colored circles on it.

5 To finish, cut a small tongue out of red felt and glue it into the mouth.

Flower Vase

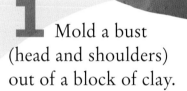

1 Mold a bust (head and shoulders) out of a block of clay.

2 Cut off the top of the head with the plastic knife.

3 Use the plastic spoon to dig the clay out from the inside of the bust's head. Leave it empty.

4 Make a nose and ears. Place them on the clay head. Let it dry.

5 Once it is dry, paint the body, eyes, mouth, and the inside of the head.

Cow

MATERIALS

White, black, and tan clay
Plastic Knife
Small dowels
Twine
Scissors
Pink paint
Paintbrush

1 Shape the body of the cow with udders out of white clay. Make a hole in the body where you can stick in a piece of twine (the tail).

2 Stick four dowels into the body for the legs, and make the hooves out of four little pieces of white clay.

3 Now shape the head and ears of the cow. Use the plastic knife to make the eyes and the snout. Attach the head to the body with another dowel.

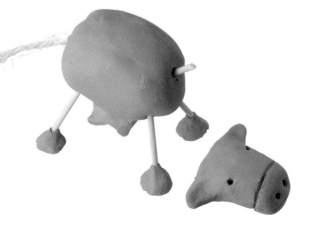

4 Make the horns out of a small roll of tan clay shaped like the letter "U." Place them on the animal's head. Finish by decorating the body with spots made out of black clay.

5 Once the cow is dry, paint the snout and the udders pink.

Fish Tray

MATERIALS

Clay
Roller
Plastic Knife
Different colors of paint
Paintbrush

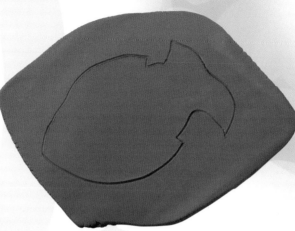

1 Prepare a thick flat piece of clay and draw the outline of a fish with a plastic knife.

2 Use the plastic knife to cut out the outline of the fish.

3 Turn up the fins, mouth, and tail a little bit in order to make the sides of the tray.

4 Draw scales on the body with a plastic knife.

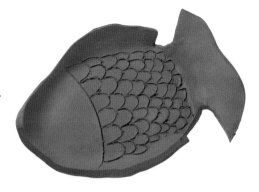

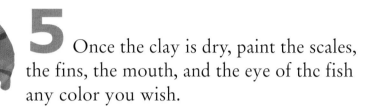

5 Once the clay is dry, paint the scales, the fins, the mouth, and the eye of the fish any color you wish.

23

Twine Doll

MATERIALS

Tan, green, brown, white, and black clay
Twine
Plastic Knife
Scissors

1 Cut two lengths of twine and make a ball of tan clay (the head) around one end, leaving some twine sticking out. Attach a little ball of clay (the nose) to the head.

2 Cut another length of twine and tie it below the head with the same amount of twine on either side. Attach clay to each end for hands.

3 Make a rectangular piece (the body) out of green clay. Push the twine for the arms and legs into the clay and cover them with more clay.

24

4 Decorate the body with three little balls of brown clay (buttons) and attach two balls of clay to the ends of the legs (feet).

5 Make the eyes out of little balls of white and black clay, and make a mouth with a plastic knife. Unravel the twine that is sticking out of the top of the head (hair). Let the doll dry.

25

Jewelry

MATERIALS

Clay
Different colors of paint
Toothpicks
Thin rope
Paintbrush

1 Make little balls of clay of different colors and shapes. You can make some by mixing different colors of clay.

2 Pierce each with toothpicks, one by one, and let them dry.

3 Once they are dry, paint some with bright colors and leave others unpainted. Let the paint dry. Take out the sticks.

26

4 Cut a piece of thin rope and string the balls of clay onto it.

5 For the clasp, tie a ball to the end of the thin rope. Tie a slip knot in the other end.

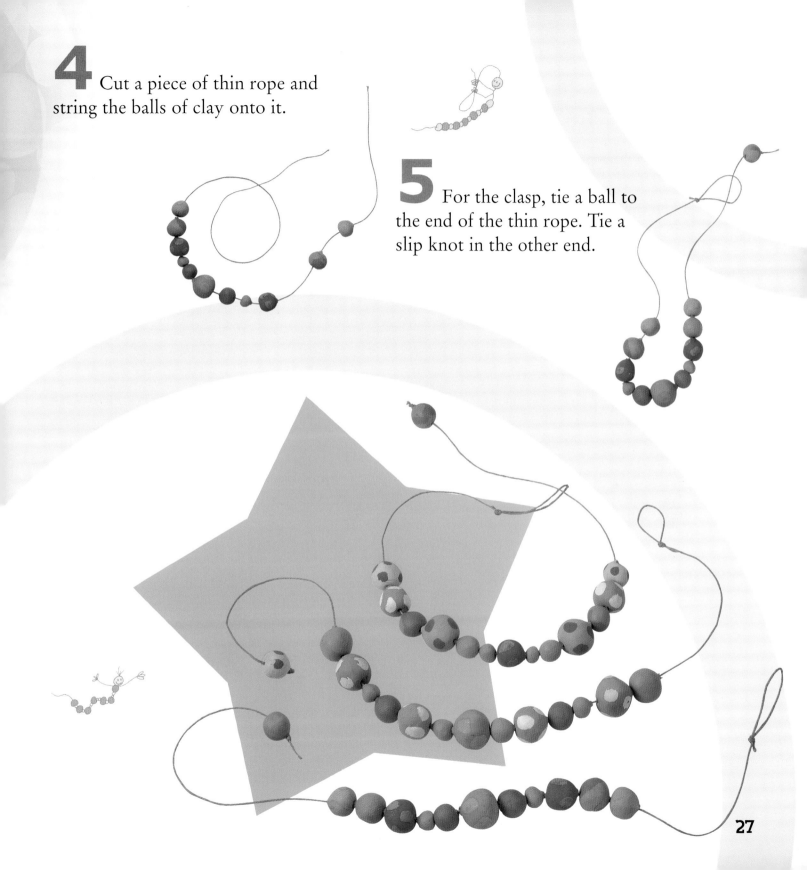

Little House

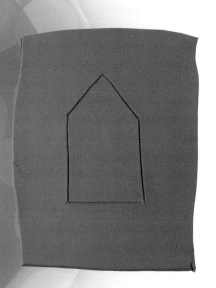

1 Flatten a piece of tan clay. Draw the outline of a house, and cut it out. This will be the base.

2 Flatten a piece of brown clay. Draw the roof of the house, and cut it out. Smooth the pieces together.

3 Flatten a piece of white clay. Draw the windows and a door, and cut them out. Attach to the base in the same way.

4 Make two little rolls of green clay, and flatten them. Place them on both sides of the door.

5 Decorate the roof and the grass with the plastic knife and make a hole at the top of the house. Once the figure is dry, put some yarn through the hole to hang it from.

Paperweight

MATERIALS

Clay
Roller
Plastic Knife
Natural raffia
Paperclip
Different colors of paint
Paintbrush

1 Mold the body and head of a figure out of clay.

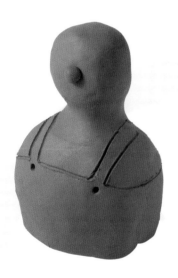

2 Draw overalls with the plastic knife and add a little ball of clay for the nose.

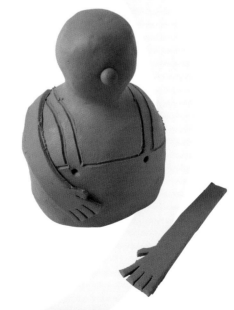

3 Draw and cut the arms and hands of the figure out of a flat piece of clay. Attach them to the body.

30

4 For the hair, cut some lengths of raffia, and tie them together. Attach them to the clay head with an open paperclip.

5 Let the figure dry, and then paint it any way you like.

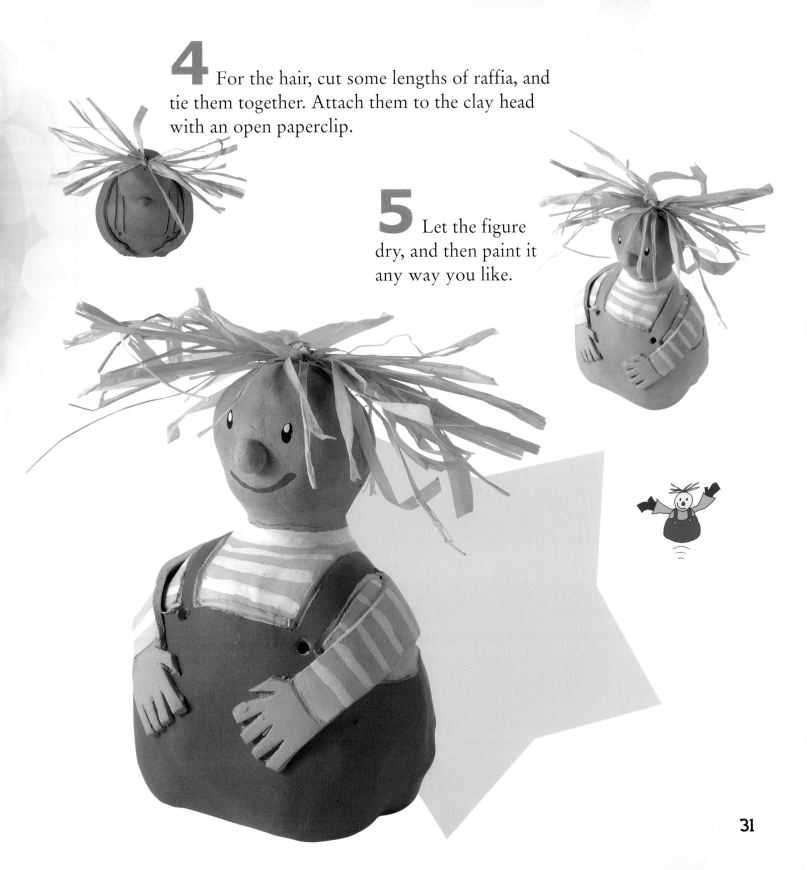

Books

Read About

Casagranda, Brigitte. *Salt Dough Fun*. Milwaukee, Wisc.: Gareth Stevens Pub., 2005.

Kirby, Huguette. *Crafts from Modeling Clay*. Mankato, Minn.: Bridgestone Books, 2003.

Wallace, Mary. *I Can Make That! Fantastic Crafts for Kids*. Toronto, Canada: Maple Tree Press, 2005.

Internet Addresses

Crafts for Kids at Enchanted Learning
<http://www.enchantedlearning.com/crafts/>

Kids Craft Weekly
<http://www.Kidscraftweekly.com/>

Index

E a s y   t o   H a r d